ALFRED, LORD TENNYSON

Mick Imlah was born in 1956 and educated at Magdalen College, Oxford. His poetry publications are *The Zoologist's Bath* and *Birthmarks*. He co-edited the *New Penguin Book of Scottish Verse* and is currently Poetry Editor of the *Times Literary Supplement*.

ALFRED, LORD TENNYSON

Poems selected by

MICK IMLAH

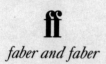

faber and faber

First published in 2004
by Faber and Faber Limited
3 Queen Square London WC1N 3AU

Photoset by Wilmaset Ltd, Birkenhead, Wirral
Printed in England by Bookmarque Ltd, Croydon

A CIP record for this book
is available from the British Library

ISBN 0–571–20700–6

10 9 8 7 6 5 4 3 2 1

Contents

Introduction

> Sunset and evening star,
> And one clear call for me!
> And let there be no moaning of the bar
> When I put out to sea ...

Tennyson wrote the hymn-like 'Crossing the Bar' in twenty minutes, on a drizzly afternoon in October 1889, aboard a boat carrying him across the Solent from Portsmouth towards his home on the Isle of Wight (the 'bar' is the extending limb of a harbour). He was eighty years old, and had barely recovered from a serious illness. When he shared the poem that evening with his loyal son Hallam, he was told, 'That is one of the most beautiful poems ever written.' (Hallam refined his remark for posterity, when compiling his *Memoir*, to 'That is the crown of your life's work.')

The poem has since been bracketed with other poems of the period which vaunt their faith in the face of death or adversity: especially Browning's 'Epilogue' to *Asolando*, which was published on the same day in December 1889 as Tennyson's *Demeter*, containing 'Crossing the Bar' – the same day, moreover, on which Browning died:

> What had I on earth to do
> With the slothful, with the mawkish, the unmanly? ...
> No at noonday in the bustle of man's work-time
> Greet the unseen with a cheer!

Yet 'slothful', 'mawkish' and 'unmanly' are all epithets which can be found in contemporary reviews of Tennyson's early poems. And the passenger of 'Crossing the Bar' – who is yet, in the euphemism, to 'put out to sea' – shares his situation, brave though he is in the face, with the classic Tennysonian character of the stranded mariner, who recurs time and again through a long career, from 'The Lotos-Eaters' (1830) and 'Ulysses'

(1833), to 'Enoch Arden' (1864) and the men on 'The Voyage of Maeldune' (1880), to name only the most literal. Readers of the lines 'When that which drew from out the boundless deep/ Turns again home' would cross over from Tennyson's own coming voyage to remember the reference to the *De Profundis* at the climax of Tennyson's Arthurian epic – 'From the great deep to the great deep he goes' ('The Passing of Arthur'). 'Mind you put my Crossing the Bar at the end of all editions of my poems,' insisted the old man, like one arranging his funeral, or stage-managing his carriage to Avalon. At the last, succeeding to the properties of his own legendary gentleman, Tennyson has outworn the trouble of being alive. What had been up with him was almost over.

Alfred Tennyson was born in 1809 at Somersby, Lincolnshire, the fourth son of the rector there. The Tennyson family history had been blighted by madness, alcoholism and opium addiction; the rector himself, in thrall to drink, had been passed over in favour of a ruthless second son. What Alfred called the 'black blood' of his kin showed itself in his own case as 'a hereditary tenderness of nerves': he was afraid of epilepsy, and susceptible to trance-like states, of the kind he was to describe in *The Princess*:

> On a sudden, in the midst of men and day,
> And while I walked and talked as heretofore,
> I seem'd to move among a world of ghosts,
> And feel myself the shadow of a dream ...

And so, while his childhood introduced him to grand houses and perfect lawns, and though at the age of thirty he still had £3,000 to throw away on a business venture, he felt himself unfortunate: as a suitor, he could claim to be thwarted by 'marriage-hindering Mammon'; and instability of several kinds seemed to be the sum of his inheritance.

Poetry, too, was in his veins. Two of his brothers, Charles (later Tennyson-Turner) and Frederick, each wrote his share of good verse. But Alfred was pulled out of Louth Grammar School at eleven, so it was only at home, by a miserable, bleary father, that his special talent was marked. And somewhere the juvenile eagerness and freedom of the mock-Jacobean drama, 'The Devil and the Lady', that he wrote when he was fourteen, with its carefree casting off to sea –

> Thereat my shallop lightly I unbound,
> Spread my white sail and rode exulting on
> The placid murmurings of each feathery wave

– thins into the feyness and anaemia and stagnation of his earliest published poems. Unfavourable reviews of Tennyson's first two books (1830 and 1832) mocked in particular that part of them which was a metrical scrapbook of girls' names: 'Claribel', 'Lilian', 'Isabel', 'Madeline', 'Marion', 'Lisette', 'Eleanore', 'My Rosalind', 'faintly smiling Adeline', 'rare pale Margaret', etc. Though these had memorable older cousins in the towered-up Lady of Shalott and the morbidly frustrated Mariana 'by the moated grange', there was no future in a poet of either sex for a style so guardedly feminine.

In 1832, Tennyson's temperament seemed inimical to his promise. The exemplary poet of that day, and incidentally Poet Laureate, was Wordsworth, whose radical innovations had been autobiography and the plain style. Tennyson's problem in presenting poems to the public was that his deepest experience was unsocial, painful, and shaming to a degree; this was no ordinary reticence. And how he might have sounded then without the dress of artifice is to be heard in an unpublished fragment of the period:

> Pierced through with knotted thorns of barren pain,
>   Deep in forethought of dark calamities,
>   Sick of the coming time and the coming woe,
> As one that tramples some volcanic plain
>   And through the yawning rifts and chasms hears
>   The scummy sulphur seething far below

And dares not to advance or to retire ...
E'en so I lay upon my bed at night:
  All my delight was gone: my hope was fresh
    No longer: and I lay with sobbing breath,
Walled round, shut up, imbarred, moaning for light,
  A carcase in the coffin of this flesh,
    Pierced through with loathly worms of utter death.

That 'coming woe' is always large on Tennyson's horizon. He was daunted by society and sex, by life as well as death; and his poems had to put on forms or metaphors which would allow him to say his 'woe' without dishonour. One valuable resource was the dramatic monologue: a speech of fictional self-disclosure, normally in Shakespearean blank verse, which he developed independently from, and rather in advance of, its more thoroughgoing exponent, Robert Browning. The difference between them was that while Browning wrote such poems to explore the dilemmas of other characters, Tennyson wrote them to mythologize his own, choosing figures from classical and other legend in 'Ulysses', 'Tithon' (remade as 'Tithonus'), and 'St Simeon Stylites': three of his very best poems of middle length, all written in 1833. But as the situation of these personae was essentially the same, marooned in helpless or perverse inactivity, they could not, as Browning's might, meet or multiply. 'Me only cruel immortality/ Consumes ...': the further development of Tennyson's poetry depended on traffic with the world, and it might yet have perished by withdrawal, had there not been an accident of grief.

Tennyson had gone up to Trinity College, Cambridge in November 1827. As an undergraduate there he won the Chancellor's Gold Medal for Poetry. But he was to leave Cambridge without taking a degree; and the real benefit of the University for him was the friendship and love of Arthur Hugh Hallam, the son of an eminent historian and himself the golden boy of his Trinity generation. Tennyson and Hallam walked the Pyrenees together in 1830: the following year,

Hallam published an essay in the *Englishman's Magazine* in extravagant praise of his friend's poems. He also fell in love with Alfred's sister; and their engagement seemed providentially to absorb and dispel the private doom of the whole family. In the autumn of 1833, news came from Vienna that Hallam was dead, of a brain haemmorhage, at twenty-two.

For fifteen years to follow, the loss of Arthur Hallam, and the hope embodied in Hallam, blended with Tennyson's constitutional depression to produce extended attacks of paralysis and complementary agitation. The exact nature of his illness – the poet himself looked back on it serenely as 'hypochondria' – is obscured by the loyalty of his friends and family. In 1840, Edward FitzGerald found him in the latest contraction of the Tennyson family home, this one at Tunbridge Wells, 'really ill in a nervous way'; in 1843, he had treatment in a hydropathic hospital near Cheltenham; friends were shocked anew at his 'pitiful' condition in 1847. But at least his sorrows were feeding now on something more substantial than self-pity. Some have marvelled at the anguish Tennyson expended on the loss of an undergraduate friendship, and inferred a homoerotic attachment; alternatively, we can read the Hallam poems (and 'Hallam' was what he called his son) as the meeting of a morbid strain with a dearly needed occasion. And in due course, the warmer reception given to the *Poems* of 1842, the award of a Civil List Pension in 1845, and the secret, intermittent development of the series of elegies for his friend, began to prepare his fortunes for a decisive turn.

There can be few better examples of the biographical phenomenon of *annus mirabilis* than Tennyson's 1850 – the midpoint of his own span, as well as of the century to which it belonged. First, in May, came the anonymous publication of, and boundless acclaim for, *In Memoriam A.H.H.*, the long poem, in lyric form, which airs and wilfully resolves the twin despairs of grief and religious doubt. The poem's success led to his being offered the title in November, after Wordsworth's death in April, of Poet Laureate. Most radical of all was his marriage in June to Emily Sellwood: a wife who had known him for twenty years, who doted on him, and rather scolded his demons (she called the black-blooded one 'Ally'). Though he had already written perhaps three quarters of the poetry on which his reputation would come to rest, he was now to enjoy four decades of a worldlier sort of success, the very heights of the stardom his age could confer.

Tennyson liked the Troubadour description of poetry as a 'gay science'; and his peers would say that English verse since Milton had known no better technician, none with so refined an instinct for the weights and measures of words and lines (a faculty in which the general reader has since lost interest). His 'ear' was commonly celebrated as a marvellous instrument, and its individual felicities collected and quoted. These included the mouthful of lines from 'Come down, O maid' –

> every sound is sweet;
> Myriads of rivulets hurrying through the lawn,
> The moan of doves in immemorial elms,
> And murmuring of innumerable bees.

– and the bathtime hullabaloo of a line from one of the Idylls, 'Oilily bubbled up the mere', which embodies the sound and sight of what is being described, but also communicates the relish of its writing.

And Tennyson was certainly pleased with his virtuosity. His friend Edward FitzGerald remembered a boating expedition on which the poet rolled out the lines from 'Morte d'Arthur' (later incorporated in 'The Passing of Arthur') on the submarine manufacture of Excalibur: 'Nine Years she wrought it, sitting in the deeps/ Upon the hidden bases of the hills', breaking off to suggest, 'Not bad that, Fitz, is it?' His private readings, which Tennyson enjoyed at least as much as his audience, were occasions for showing off. FitzGerald again, on the ascetical monologue 'St Simeon Stylites': 'This is one of the

Poems A.T. would read with grotesque Grimness, especially at such passages as "Coughs, Aches, Stitches, etc.", laughing aloud at times.'

When Tennyson's poetry is at its best, these lavish gifts are in balance with the prompting of his wounds and fears; but in the calm of his maturity their display could seem like facility. FitzGerald saw this as early as *In Memoriam*, observing that the poem, while 'full of finest things', had 'that air of being evolved by a Poetical Machine of the highest order'. We get more of what the Victorians called 'Parnassian' – poetry produced by the ream under low pressure and generalized outlook – as Tennyson began to shape a career.

This meant, first, a broadening of his subject-matter, which met with some reward. He produced poems in the Lincolnshire dialect, like 'The Northern Farmer' pieces, increasingly valued for their novelty, their regional cachet and relaxed naturalism. There are poems of friendship, mostly in letter form, all finely decorous and graced with feeling, of which several examples are included in this selection. And there are the identifiably 'Laureate' poems, the most successful ever written in that discredited genre: paeans to heroes of English history and prehistory, responses, like 'The Charge of the Light Brigade', to the day's events, but also the more demanding and (in the execution) aptly ceremonial 'Ode on the Death of the Duke of Wellington'.

The Poet Laureate of the foremost national power of the day was famously short-sighted (one reason why his landscapes were so often 'glimmering'), and that might be said to apply also to his sympathies. He felt with England rather than mankind; if he especially deplored the 'red fool-fury' of the French, even the Greater Britain, incorporating 'the blind hysterics of the Celt', could provoke his conservative distaste. In comparison with his Romantic predecessors, he shunned the forward look, and if he favoured 'liberty' it was by gradations, in a land 'Where Freedom slowly broadens down/ From precedent to precedent'. The best remedy he can come up with for the corruption of the capitalist system, as discovered by the manic narrator of *Maud*, is war.

Yet within his limits, which did not extend to conditions in the mill towns, Tennyson had always busied himself to look in touch with the present day. His self-consciousness on this front produces curious effects in the poems he grouped under the title 'English Idyls' ('Edwin Morris' is included here), where fragments of the contemporary, in particular the new geology, are presented like museum pieces. In 'Audley Court', picnickers enjoy a 'pasty costly-made/ Where quail and pigeon, lark and leveret lay/ Like fossils of the rock'; in 'The Golden Year', an old Welshman ponders the seasons: 'He spoke; and high above, I heard them blast/ The steep slate-quarry'. Again, the fashionable side of Tennyson devised modern frames for legendary narratives, things like the apologies with which later poets dress their wares at readings: 'The Epic', a 'prelude of disparagement' which provides an amiable fireside context for the Homeric 'Morte d'Arthur'; or the preamble to a poem about Lady Godiva, beginning, like Philip Larkin at his flattest, 'I waited for the train at Coventry . . .' Still, the old-style poems are the point; not the insinuating prologues.

These shuffles of address are one sign of Tennyson knowing exactly what he was good at, and how this differed from what he might like to write. He told a friend, James Knowles,

> I soon found that if I meant to make any mark at all it must be by shortness, for all the men before me had been so diffuse [he was thinking of Wordsworth], and all the big things had been done. To get the workmanship as nearly perfect as possible is the best chance for going down the stream of time. A small vessel on fine lines is likely to float further than a great raft.

The choice of the small vessel was not quite so strategic: if T. S. Eliot's verdict that 'For narrative Tennyson had no gift at all' is an exaggeration, Tennyson knew that his genius was for stillness, not for action. Yet the poet coveted the major status that could only be conferred by larger structures. Hence, each of the four 'big things' of his maturity hazards, with conscious and sometimes laborious originality, a new combination of forms; and each of them registers a total wordcount that belies the local scale of its most memorable effects.

The first of these, *The Princess* (1847), while still striking every reader as too long, deliberately sheds the responsibilities of the long poem, in all manner of disclaimers that begin with the protective modesty of its subtitle, 'A Medley'. In the poem's conclusion, the narrator wonders afresh what kind of poem (were he to make it into a poem!) would suit the material he has just put before us: should it be burlesque or epic? Should he aim to satisfy 'the mockers' in his audience, or the realists?

And I, betwixt them both, to please them both,
And yet to give the story as it rose,
I moved as in a strange diagonal,
And maybe neither pleased myself nor them.

Indeed, the poem's chief distinction by far are its ten interpolated lyrics or arias, 'Tears, idle tears ...', 'Now sleeps the crimson petal ...' and the others, whose place is dismissively contrived – 'And let the ladies sing us, if they will,/ From time to time, some ballad or a song' – and whose millions of readers have generally met them relieved of their context. These beautiful luxuries are inset like gems in a narrative – about a women's university, incidentally – that is speculative, whimsical, rambling, unsure of its trajectory or success.

Succeeding ventures were no less a matter, formally speaking, of seeking out the 'strange diagonal'. *In Memoriam* (1850) is made up of as many as 132 sections, each of several quatrains in the same simple stanza form and humble diction: to the connoisseur of these things, it is not least an album of the changes that can be rung out of a single lyric idea. But the poem repeatedly questions whether the physical flimsiness of its parts, 'Short swallow-flights of song, that dip/ Their wings in tears, and skim away', are up to the philosophical labour, the engagement with death and the Universe, that it sets out to accomplish. By contrast, the book-length poem *Maud* (1855) unleashes a whole range of different lyric forms, intended to simulate the fluctuating and contending moods of the narrator, an unnamed madman. In *Maud*, the story is shadowed rather than told: since the action occurs between the 'scenes', and is erratically reported, the puzzle is what really happens – a murder, we suppose. A contemporary reviewer, Ralph Mann, coined the genre 'monodrama' to define the poem; Tennyson immediately adopted the suggestion as a subtitle, and nothing else has been called a 'monodrama' since.

Then there was *Idylls of the King*: the project, developed over forty years, that Tennyson considered (especially before he had finished it) his magnum opus: here the battle between the big scheme and the little vessel is enacted in the title. Tennyson's own choice of title, both for the four-book volume published in 1859 and for the final scheme of 1885 that evolved around it, posits a blend of the matter and proportions of epic with the local techniques of the miniature. The *Idylls* of 1885 appeared 'In Twelve Books', in blank verse, with Homeric formulae, a distinct moral design, and an allegorical drift; on the other hand, Tennyson explicitly rejected the term 'epic' as a 'misnomer', and wrote pedantically of his alternative definition, 'I spelt my Idylls with two *l*s mainly to divide them from the ordinary pastoral idyls usually spelt with one *l*'. Moreover, these are not *The Idylls*, as if they were exhaustive, but *Idylls*, a selection of the possible. The work is at once one poem, and twelve, or neither; both vastly ambitious and sweet with the pathos of inadequacy.

The *Idylls* will never again be read for its (or their) wooden dialogue, for its moral design or the tentative gimmicks of its narrative – if it ever was. 'I can only read it for the sake of the next lollipop', complained one contemporary, 'but the lollipops when they come are delicious.' The pick of those treats are the moments, still, of trance: whether they strike Arthur, or

Guinevere, or Lancelot ('Round whose sick head all night, like birds of prey,/ The words of Arthur flying shrieked'), or Merlin:

So dark a forethought rolled about his brain,
As on a dull day in an ocean cave
The blind wave feeling round his long sea-hall
In silence ...

For these are not illuminations of a particular character: the reader's experience in every case is of the same single mind reeling in its isolation. The lines of Tennyson's longer poems, like the mass of his shorter ones, can be separated almost categorically into the live (for this is how it strikes the reader) and the manufactured. And the essential energy, whatever fabulous guise it assumes, whatever the landscape it echoes in, is privately generated; it is the poet's sadness.

In consequence of such things, the word 'from', indicating an extract, is unusually prevalent on the contents page of this volume. But no one says of Tennyson that you need to read the whole to appreciate the parts. Just as the *Idylls* is a pageant whose longueurs justify its sudden depths, *Maud* a contrivance for the venting of buried steam, and *The Princess* an elaborate cabinet setting for its sublime lyrics, the whole of Tennyson's long career is a shelter for the sensational revelation of his melancholy. The 'life's work' of which 'Crossing the Bar' may be called the 'crown' is the practice – covert at times – of a lyric vocation. Tennyson stands as he intended, as a great poet of proven range and formidable stamina: but one who is none the less ideally read in selection.

MICK IMLAH

ALFRED, LORD TENNYSON

The Kraken

Below the thunders of the upper deep;
Far, far beneath in the abysmal sea,
His ancient, dreamless, uninvaded sleep
The Kraken sleepeth: faintest sunlights flee
About his shadowy sides: above him swell
Huge sponges of millennial growth and height;
And far away into the sickly light,
From many a wondrous grot and secret cell
Unnumbered and enormous polypi
Winnow with giant arms the slumbering green.
There hath he lain for ages and will lie
Battening upon huge seaworms in his sleep,
Until the latter fire shall heat the deep;
Then once by man and angels to be seen,
In roaring he shall rise and on the surface die.

Song

I

A spirit haunts the year's last hours
Dwelling amid these yellowing bowers:
    To himself he talks;
For at eventide, listening earnestly,
At his work you may hear him sob and sigh
    In the walks;
    Earthward he boweth the heavy stalks
Of the mouldering flowers:
  Heavily hangs the broad sunflower
    Over its grave i' the earth so chilly;
  Heavily hangs the hollyhock,
    Heavily hangs the tiger-lily.

II

The air is damp, and hushed, and close,
As a sick man's room when he taketh repose
    An hour before death;
My very heart faints and my whole soul grieves
At the moist rich smell of the rotting leaves,
    And the breath
    Of the fading edges of box beneath,
And the year's last rose.
  Heavily hangs the broad sunflower
    Over its grave i' the earth so chilly;
  Heavily hangs the hollyhock,
    Heavily hangs the tiger-lily.

Mariana

Mariana in the moated grange – Measure for Measure

With blackest moss the flower-plots
   Were thickly crusted, one and all:
The rusted nails fell from the knots
   That held the pear to the gable-wall.
The broken sheds looked sad and strange:
   Unlifted was the clinking latch;
   Weeded and worn the ancient thatch
Upon the lonely moated grange.
     She only said, 'My life is dreary,
       He cometh not,' she said;
     She said, 'I am aweary, aweary,
       I would that I were dead!'

Her tears fell with the dews at even;
   Her tears fell ere the dews were dried;
She could not look on the sweet heaven,
   Either at morn or eventide.
After the flitting of the bats,
   When thickest dark did trance the sky,
   She drew her casement-curtain by,
And glanced athwart the glooming flats.
     She only said, 'The night is dreary,
       He cometh not,' she said;
     She said, 'I am aweary, aweary,
       I would that I were dead!'

Upon the middle of the night,
   Waking she heard the night-fowl crow:
The cock sung out an hour ere light:
   From the dark fen the oxen's low
Came to her: without hope of change,
   In sleep she seemed to walk forlorn,
   Till cold winds woke the gray-eyed morn

About the lonely moated grange.
    She only said, 'The day is dreary,
      He cometh not,' she said;
    She said, 'I am aweary, aweary,
      I would that I were dead!'

About a stone-cast from the wall
  A sluice with blackened waters slept,
And o'er it many, round and small,
  The clustered marish-mosses crept.
Hard by a poplar shook alway,
  All silver-green with gnarlèd bark:
  For leagues no other tree did mark
The level waste, the rounding gray.
    She only said, 'My life is dreary,
      He cometh not,' she said;
    She said, 'I am aweary, aweary,
      I would that I were dead!'

And ever when the moon was low,
  And the shrill winds were up and away,
In the white curtain, to and fro,
  She saw the gusty shadow sway.
But when the moon was very low,
  And wild winds bound within their cell,
  The shadow of the poplar fell
Upon her bed, across her brow.
    She only said, 'The night is dreary,
      He cometh not,' she said;
    She said, 'I am aweary, aweary,
      I would that I were dead!'

All day within the dreamy house,
  The doors upon their hinges creaked;
The blue fly sung in the pane; the mouse
  Behind the mouldering wainscot shrieked,
Or from the crevice peered about.

Old faces glimmered through the doors,
  Old footsteps trod the upper floors,
Old voices called her from without.
    She only said, 'My life is dreary,
      He cometh not,' she said;
    She said, 'I am aweary, aweary,
      I would that I were dead!'

The sparrow's chirrup on the roof,
  The slow clock ticking, and the sound
Which to the wooing wind aloof
  The poplar made, did all confound
Her sense; but most she loathed the hour
  When the thick-moted sunbeam lay
  Athwart the chambers, and the day
Was sloping toward his western bower.
    Then, said she, 'I am very dreary,
      He will not come,' she said;
    She wept, 'I am aweary, aweary,
      Oh God, that I were dead!'

The Lotos-Eaters

'Courage!' he said, and pointed toward the land,
'This mounting wave will roll us shoreward soon.'
In the afternoon they came unto a land
In which it seemèd always afternoon.
All round the coast the languid air did swoon,
Breathing like one that hath a weary dream.
Full-faced above the valley stood the moon;
And like a downward smoke, the slender stream
Along the cliff to fall and pause and fall did seem.

A land of streams! some, like a downward smoke,
Slow-dropping veils of thinnest lawn, did go;
And some through wavering lights and shadows broke,
Rolling a slumbrous sheet of foam below.
They saw the gleaming river seaward flow
From the inner land: far off, three mountain-tops,
Three silent pinnacles of agèd snow,
Stood sunset-flushed: and, dewed with showery drops,
Up-clomb the shadowy pine above the woven copse.

The charmèd sunset lingered low adown
In the red West: through mountain clefts the dale
Was seen far inland, and the yellow down
Bordered with palm, and many a winding vale
And meadow, set with slender galingale;
A land where all things always seemed the same!
And round about the keel with faces pale,
Dark faces pale against that rosy flame,
The mild-eyed melancholy Lotos-eaters came.

Branches they bore of that enchanted stem,
Laden with flower and fruit, whereof they gave
To each, but whoso did receive of them,
And taste, to him the gushing of the wave

Far far away did seem to mourn and rave
On alien shores; and if his fellow spake,
His voice was thin, as voices from the grave;
And deep-asleep he seemed, yet all awake,
And music in his ears his beating heart did make.

They sat them down upon the yellow sand,
Between the sun and moon upon the shore;
And sweet it was to dream of Fatherland,
Of child, and wife, and slave; but evermore
Most weary seemed the sea, weary the oar,
Weary the wandering fields of barren foam.
Then some one said, 'We will return no more;'
And all at once they sang, 'Our island home
Is far beyond the wave; we will no longer roam.'

CHORIC SONG

I

There is sweet music here that softer falls
Than petals from blown roses on the grass,
Or night-dews on still waters between walls
Of shadowy granite, in a gleaming pass;
Music that gentlier on the spirit lies,
Than tired eyelids upon tired eyes;
Music that brings sweet sleep down from the blissful skies.
Here are cool mosses deep,
And through the moss the ivies creep,
And in the stream the long-leaved flowers weep,
And from the craggy ledge the poppy hangs in sleep.

II

Why are we weighed upon with heaviness,
And utterly consumed with sharp distress,
While all things else have rest from weariness?
All things have rest: why should we toil alone,
We only toil, who are the first of things,

And make perpetual moan,
Still from one sorrow to another thrown:
Nor ever fold our wings,
And cease from wanderings,
Nor steep our brows in slumber's holy balm;
Nor harken what the inner spirit sings,
'There is no joy but calm!'
Why should we only toil, the roof and crown of things?

III

Lo! in the middle of the wood,
The folded leaf is wooed from out the bud
With winds upon the branch, and there
Grows green and broad, and takes no care,
Sun-steeped at noon, and in the moon
Nightly dew-fed; and turning yellow
Falls, and floats adown the air.
Lo! sweetened with the summer light,
The full-juiced apple, waxing over-mellow,
Drops in a silent autumn night.
All its allotted length of days,
The flower ripens in its place,
Ripens and fades, and falls, and hath no toil,
Fast-rooted in the fruitful soil.

IV

Hateful is the dark-blue sky,
Vaulted o'er the dark-blue sea.
Death is the end of life; ah, why
Should life all labour be?
Let us alone. Time driveth onward fast,
And in a little while our lips are dumb.
Let us alone. What is it that will last?
All things are taken from us, and become
Portions and parcels of the dreadful Past.
Let us alone. What pleasure can we have
To war with evil? Is there any peace

In ever climbing up the climbing wave?
All things have rest, and ripen toward the grave
In silence; ripen, fall and cease:
Give us long rest or death, dark death, or dreamful ease.

V

How sweet it were, hearing the downward stream,
With half-shut eyes ever to seem
Falling asleep in a half-dream!
To dream and dream, like yonder amber light,
Which will not leave the myrrh-bush on the height;
To hear each other's whispered speech;
Eating the Lotos day by day,
To watch the crisping ripples on the beach,
And tender curving lines of creamy spray;
To lend our hearts and spirits wholly
To the influence of mild-minded melancholy;
To muse and brood and live again in memory,
With those old faces of our infancy
Heaped over with a mound of grass,
Two handfuls of white dust, shut in an urn of brass!

VI

Dear is the memory of our wedded lives,
And dear the last embraces of our wives
And their warm tears: but all hath suffered change:
For surely now our household hearths are cold:
Our sons inherit us: our looks are strange:
And we should come like ghosts to trouble joy.
Or else the island princes over-bold
Have eat our substance, and the minstrel sings
Before them of the ten years' war in Troy,
And our great deeds, as half-forgotten things.
Is there confusion in the little isle?
Let what is broken so remain.
The Gods are hard to reconcile:
'Tis hard to settle order once again.

There *is* confusion worse than death,
Trouble on trouble, pain on pain,
Long labour unto agèd breath,
Sore task to hearts worn out by many wars
And eyes grown dim with gazing on the pilot-stars.

VII

But, propt on beds of amaranth and moly,
How sweet (while warm airs lull us, blowing lowly)
With half-dropt eyelid still,
Beneath a heaven dark and holy,
To watch the long bright river drawing slowly
His waters from the purple hill –
To hear the dewy echoes calling
From cave to cave through the thick-twinèd vine –
To watch the emerald-coloured water falling
Through many a woven acanthus-wreath divine!
Only to hear and see the far-off sparkling brine,
Only to hear were sweet, stretched out beneath the pine.

VIII

The Lotos blooms below the barren peak:
The Lotos blows by every winding creek:
All day the wind breathes low with mellower tone:
Through every hollow cave and alley lone
Round and round the spicy downs the yellow Lotos-dust is
    blown.
We have had enough of action, and of motion we,
Rolled to starboard, rolled to larboard, when the surge was
    seething free,
Where the wallowing monster spouted his foam-fountains in
    the sea.
Let us swear an oath, and keep it with an equal mind,
In the hollow Lotos-land to live and lie reclined
On the hills like Gods together, careless of mankind.
For they lie beside their nectar, and the bolts are hurled
Far below them in the valleys, and the clouds are lightly curled

Round their golden houses, girdled with the gleaming world:
Where they smile in secret, looking over wasted lands,
Blight and famine, plague and earthquake, roaring deeps and
    fiery sands,
Clanging fights, and flaming towns, and sinking ships, and
    praying hands.
But they smile, they find a music centred in a doleful song
Steaming up, a lamentation and an ancient tale of wrong,
Like a tale of little meaning though the words are strong;
Chanted from an ill-used race of men that cleave the soil,
Sow the seed, and reap the harvest with enduring toil,
Storing yearly little dues of wheat, and wine and oil;
Till they perish and they suffer – some, 'tis whispered – down
    in hell
Suffer endless anguish, others in Elysian valleys dwell,
Resting weary limbs at last on beds of asphodel.
Surely, surely, slumber is more sweet than toil, the shore
Than labour in the deep mid-ocean, wind and wave and oar;
Oh rest ye, brother mariners, we will not wander more.

Ulysses

It little profits that an idle king,
By this still hearth, among these barren crags,
Matched with an agèd wife, I mete and dole
Unequal laws unto a savage race,
That hoard, and sleep, and feed, and know not me.

I cannot rest from travel: I will drink
Life to the lees: all times I have enjoyed
Greatly, have suffered greatly, both with those
That loved me, and alone; on shore, and when
Through scudding drifts the rainy Hyades
Vext the dim sea: I am become a name;
For always roaming with a hungry heart
Much have I seen and known; cities of men
And manners, climates, councils, governments,
Myself not least, but honoured of them all;
And drunk delight of battle with my peers,
Far on the ringing plains of windy Troy.

I am a part of all that I have met;
Yet all experience is an arch wherethrough
Gleams that untravelled world, whose margin fades
For ever and for ever when I move.
How dull it is to pause, to make an end,
To rust unburnished, not to shine in use!
As though to breathe were life. Life piled on life
Were all too little, and of one to me
Little remains: but every hour is saved
From that eternal silence, something more,
A bringer of new things; and vile it were
For some three suns to store and hoard myself,
And this gray spirit yearning in desire
To follow knowledge like a sinking star,
Beyond the utmost bound of human thought.

This is my son, mine own Telemachus,
To whom I leave the sceptre and the isle –
Well-loved of me, discerning to fulfil
This labour, by slow prudence to make mild
A rugged people, and through soft degrees
Subdue them to the useful and the good.
Most blameless is he, centred in the sphere
Of common duties, decent not to fail
In offices of tenderness, and pay
Meet adoration to my household gods,
When I am gone. He works his work, I mine.

There lies the port; the vessel puffs her sail:
There gloom the dark broad seas. My mariners,
Souls that have toiled, and wrought, and thought with me –
That ever with a frolic welcome took
The thunder and the sunshine, and opposed
Free hearts, free foreheads – you and I are old;
Old age hath yet his honour and his toil;
Death closes all: but something ere the end,
Some work of noble note, may yet be done,
Not unbecoming men that strove with Gods.
The lights begin to twinkle from the rocks:
The long day wanes: the slow moon climbs: the deep
Moans round with many voices. Come, my friends,
'Tis not too late to seek a newer world.
Push off, and sitting well in order smite
The sounding furrows; for my purpose holds
To sail beyond the sunset, and the baths
Of all the western stars, until I die.
It may be that the gulfs will wash us down:
It may be we shall touch the Happy Isles,
And see the great Achilles, whom we knew.
Though much is taken, much abides; and though
We are not now that strength which in old days
Moved earth and heaven; that which we are, we are;

One equal temper of heroic hearts,
Made weak by time and fate, but strong in will
To strive, to seek, to find, and not to yield.

Tithonus

The woods decay, the woods decay and fall,
The vapours weep their burthen to the ground,
Man comes and tills the field and lies beneath,
And after many a summer dies the swan.
Me only cruel immortality
Consumes: I wither slowly in thine arms,
Here at the quiet limit of the world,
A white-haired shadow roaming like a dream
The ever-silent spaces of the East,
Far-folded mists, and gleaming halls of morn.

   Alas! for this gray shadow, once a man –
So glorious in his beauty and thy choice,
Who madest him thy chosen, that he seemed
To his great heart none other than a God!
I asked thee, 'Give me immortality.'
Then didst thou grant mine asking with a smile,
Like wealthy men who care not how they give.
But thy strong Hours indignant worked their wills,
And beat me down and marred and wasted me,
And though they could not end me, left me maimed
To dwell in presence of immortal youth,
Immortal age beside immortal youth,
And all I was, in ashes. Can thy love,
Thy beauty, make amends, though even now,
Close over us, the silver star, thy guide,
Shines in those tremulous eyes that fill with tears
To hear me? Let me go: take back thy gift:
Why should a man desire in any way
To vary from the kindly race of men,
Or pass beyond the goal of ordinance
Where all should pause, as is most meet for all?

A soft air fans the cloud apart; there comes
A glimpse of that dark world where I was born.
Once more the old mysterious glimmer steals
From thy pure brows, and from thy shoulders pure,
And bosom beating with a heart renewed.
Thy cheek begins to redden through the gloom,
Thy sweet eyes brighten slowly close to mine,
Ere yet they blind the stars, and the wild team
Which love thee, yearning for thy yoke, arise,
And shake the darkness from their loosened manes,
And beat the twilight into flakes of fire.

Lo! ever thus thou growest beautiful
In silence, then before thine answer given
Departest, and thy tears are on my cheek.

Why wilt thou ever scare me with thy tears,
And make me tremble lest a saying learnt,
In days far-off, on that dark earth, be true?
'The Gods themselves cannot recall their gifts.'

Ay me! ay me! with what another heart
In days far-off, and with what other eyes
I used to watch – if I be he that watched –
The lucid outline forming round thee; saw
The dim curls kindle into sunny rings;
Changed with thy mystic change, and felt my blood
Glow with the glow that slowly crimsoned all
Thy presence and thy portals, while I lay,
Mouth, forehead, eyelids, growing dewy-warm
With kisses balmier than half-opening buds
Of April, and could hear the lips that kissed
Whispering I knew not what of wild and sweet,
Like that strange song I heard Apollo sing,
While Ilion like a mist rose into towers.

Yet hold me not for ever in thine East:
How can my nature longer mix with thine?

Coldly thy rosy shadows bathe me, cold
Are all thy lights, and cold my wrinkled feet
Upon thy glimmering thresholds, when the steam
Floats up from those dim fields about the homes
Of happy men that have the power to die,
And grassy barrows of the happier dead.
Release me, and restore me to the ground;
Thou seëst all things, thou wilt see my grave:
Thou wilt renew thy beauty morn by morn;
I earth in earth forget these empty courts,
And thee returning on thy silver wheels.

St Simeon Stylites

Although I be the basest of mankind,
From scalp to sole one slough and crust of sin,
Unfit for earth, unfit for heaven, scarce meet
For troops of devils, mad with blasphemy,
I will not cease to grasp the hope I hold
Of saintdom, and to clamour, mourn and sob,
Battering the gates of heaven with storms of prayer,
Have mercy, Lord, and take away my sin.

  Let this avail, just, dreadful, mighty God,
This not be all in vain, that thrice ten years,
Thrice multiplied by superhuman pangs,
In hungers and in thirsts, fevers and cold,
In coughs, aches, stitches, ulcerous throes and cramps,
A sign betwixt the meadow and the cloud,
Patient on this tall pillar I have borne
Rain, wind, frost, heat, hail, damp, and sleet, and snow;
And I had hoped, that ere this period closed
Thou wouldst have caught me up into thy rest,
Denying not these weather-beaten limbs
The meed of saints, the white robe and the palm.

  O take the meaning, Lord: I do not breathe,
Not whisper, any murmur of complaint.
Pain heaped ten-hundred-fold to this, were still
Less burthen, by ten-hundred-fold, to bear,
Than were those lead-like tons of sin that crushed
My spirit flat before thee.
                              O Lord, Lord,
Thou knowest I bore this better at the first,
For I was strong and hale of body then;
And though my teeth, which now are dropt away,
Would chatter with the cold, and all my beard
Was tagged with icy fringes in the moon,

I drowned the whoopings of the owl with sound
Of pious hymns and psalms, and sometimes saw
An angel stand and watch me, as I sang.
Now am I feeble grown; my end draws nigh;
I hope my end draws nigh: half deaf I am,
So that I scarce can hear the people hum
About the column's base, and almost blind,
And scarce can recognise the fields I know;
And both my thighs are rotted with the dew;
Yet cease I not to clamour and to cry,
While my stiff spine can hold my weary head,
Till all my limbs drop piecemeal from the stone,
Have mercy, mercy: take away my sin.

O Jesus, if thou wilt not save my soul,
Who may be saved? who is it may be saved?
Who may be made a saint, if I fail here?
Show me the man hath suffered more than I.
For did not all thy martyrs die one death?
For either they were stoned, or crucified,
Or burned in fire, or boiled in oil, or sawn
In twain beneath the ribs; but I die here
Today, and whole years long, a life of death.
Bear witness; if I could have found a way
(And heedfully I sifted all my thought)
More slowly-painful to subdue this home
Of sin, my flesh, which I despise and hate,
I had not stinted practice, O my God.

For not alone this pillar-punishment,
Not this alone I bore: but while I lived
In the white convent down the valley there,
For many weeks about my loins I wore
The rope that haled the buckets from the well,
Twisted as tight as I could knot the noose;
And spake not of it to a single soul,
Until the ulcer, eating through my skin,

Betrayed my secret penance, so that all
My brethren marvelled greatly. More than this
I bore, whereof, O God, thou knowest all.

Three winters, that my soul might grow to thee,
I lived up there on yonder mountain side.
My right leg chained into the crag, I lay
Pent in a roofless close of ragged stones;
Inswathed sometimes in wandering mist, and twice
Blacked with thy branding thunder, and sometimes
Sucking the damps for drink, and eating not,
Except the spare chance-gift of those that came
To touch my body and be healed, and live:
And they say then that I worked miracles,
Whereof my fame is loud amongst mankind,
Cured lameness, palsies, cancers. Thou, O God,
Knowest alone whether this was or no.
Have mercy, mercy! cover all my sin.

Then, that I might be more alone with thee,
Three years I lived upon a pillar, high
Six cubits, and three years on one of twelve;
And twice three years I crouched on one that rose
Twenty by measure; last of all, I grew
Twice ten long weary weary years to this,
That numbers forty cubits from the soil.

I think that I have borne as much as this —
Or else I dream — and for so long a time,
If I may measure time by yon slow light,
And this high dial, which my sorrow crowns —
So much — even so.

     And yet I know not well,
For that the evil ones come here, and say,
'Fall down, O Simeon: thou hast suffered long
For ages and for ages!' then they prate
Of penances I cannot have gone through,

Perplexing me with lies; and oft I fall,
Maybe for months, in such blind lethargies
That Heaven, and Earth, and Time are choked.

                                        But yet
Bethink thee, Lord, while thou and all the saints
Enjoy themselves in heaven, and men on earth
House in the shade of comfortable roofs,
Sit with their wives by fires, eat wholesome food,
And wear warm clothes, and even beasts have stalls,
I, 'tween the spring and downfall of the light,
Bow down one thousand and two hundred times,
To Christ, the Virgin Mother, and the saints;
Or in the night, after a little sleep,
I wake: the chill stars sparkle; I am wet
With drenching dews, or stiff with crackling frost.
I wear an undressed goatskin on my back;
A grazing iron collar grinds my neck;
And in my weak, lean arms I lift the cross,
And strive and wrestle with thee till I die:
O mercy, mercy! wash away my sin.

    O Lord, thou knowest what a man I am;
A sinful man, conceived and born in sin:
'Tis their own doing; this is none of mine;
Lay it not to me. Am I to blame for this,
That here come those that worship me? Ha! ha!
They think that I am somewhat. What am I?
The silly people take me for a saint,
And bring me offerings of fruit and flowers:
And I, in truth (thou wilt bear witness here)
Have all in all endured as much, and more
Than many just and holy men, whose names
Are registered and calendared for saints.

    Good people, you do ill to kneel to me.
What is it I can have done to merit this?
I am a sinner viler than you all.

It may be I have wrought some miracles,
And cured some halt and maimed; but what of that?
It may be, no one, even among the saints,
May match his pains with mine; but what of that?
Yet do not rise; for you may look on me,
And in your looking you may kneel to God.
Speak! is there any of you halt or maimed?
I think you know I have some power with Heaven
From my long penance: let him speak his wish.

   Yes, I can heal him. Power goes forth from me.
They say that they are healed. Ah, hark! they shout
'St Simeon Stylites.' Why, if so,
God reaps a harvest in me. O my soul,
God reaps a harvest in thee. If this be,
Can I work miracles and not be saved?
This is not told of any. They were saints.
It cannot be but that I shall be saved;
Yea, crowned a saint. They shout, 'Behold a saint!'
And lower voices saint me from above.
Courage, St Simeon! This dull chrysalis
Cracks into shining wings, and hope ere death
Spreads more and more and more, that God hath now
Sponged and made blank of crimeful record all
My mortal archives.
                              O my sons, my sons,
I, Simeon of the pillar, by surname
Stylites, among men; I, Simeon,
The watcher on the column till the end;
I, Simeon, whose brain the sunshine bakes;
I, whose bald brows in silent hours become
Unnaturally hoar with rime, do now
From my high nest of penance here proclaim
That Pontius and Iscariot by my side
Showed like fair seraphs. On the coals I lay,
A vessel full of sin: all hell beneath

Made me boil over. Devils plucked my sleeve,
Abaddon and Asmodeus caught at me.
I smote them with the cross; they swarmed again.
In bed like monstrous apes they crushed my chest:
They flapped my light out as I read: I saw
Their faces grow between me and my book;
With colt-like whinny and with hoggish whine
They burst my prayer. Yet this way was left,
And by this way I 'scaped them. Mortify
Your flesh, like me, with scourges and with thorns;
Smite, shrink not, spare not. If it may be, fast
Whole Lents, and pray. I hardly, with slow steps,
With slow, faint steps, and much exceeding pain,
Have scrambled past those pits of fire, that still
Sing in mine ears. But yield not me the praise:
God only through his bounty hath thought fit,
Among the powers and princes of this world,
To make me an example to mankind,
Which few can reach to. Yet I do not say
But that a time may come – yea, even now,
Now, now, his footsteps smite the threshold stairs
Of life – I say, that time is at the doors
When you may worship me without reproach;
For I will leave my relics in your land,
And you may carve a shrine about my dust,
And burn a fragrant lamp before my bones,
When I am gathered to the glorious saints.

While I spake then, a sting of shrewdest pain,
Ran shrivelling through me, and a cloudlike change,
In passing, with a grosser film made thick
These heavy, horny eyes. The end! the end!
Surely the end! What's here? a shape, a shade,
A flash of light. Is that the angel there
That holds a crown? Come, blessèd brother, come.
I know thy glittering face. I waited long;

My brows are ready. What! deny it now?
Nay, draw, draw, draw nigh. So I clutch it. Christ!
'Tis gone: 'tis here again; the crown! the crown!
So now 'tis fitted on and grows to me,
And from it melt the dews of Paradise,
Sweet! sweet! spikenard, and balm, and frankincense.
Ah! let me not be fooled, sweet saints: I trust
That I am whole, and clean, and meet for Heaven.

Speak, if there be a priest, a man of God,
Among you there, and let him presently
Approach, and lean a ladder on the shaft,
And climbing up into my airy home,
Deliver me the blessèd sacrament;
For by the warning of the Holy Ghost,
I prophesy that I shall die tonight,
A quarter before twelve.
                              But thou, O Lord,
Aid all this foolish people; let them take
Example, pattern: lead them to thy light.

'Break, break, break'

Break, break, break,
　　On thy cold gray stones, O Sea!
And I would that my tongue could utter
　　The thoughts that arise in me.

O well for the fisherman's boy,
　　That he shouts with his sister at play!
O well for the sailor lad,
　　That he sings in his boat on the bay!

And the stately ships go on
　　To their haven under the hill;
But O for the touch of a vanished hand,
　　And the sound of a voice that is still!

Break, break, break,
　　At the foot of thy crags, O Sea!
But the tender grace of a day that is dead
　　Will never come back to me.

Godiva

I waited for the train at Coventry;
I hung with grooms and porters on the bridge,
To watch the three tall spires; and there I shaped
The city's ancient legend into this: –

Not only we, the latest seed of Time,
New men, that in the flying of a wheel
Cry down the past, not only we, that prate
Of rights and wrongs, have loved the people well,
And loathed to see them overtaxed; but she
Did more, and underwent, and overcame,
The woman of a thousand summers back,
Godiva, wife to that grim Earl, who ruled
In Coventry: for when he laid a tax
Upon his town, and all the mothers brought
Their children, clamouring, 'If we pay, we starve!'
She sought her lord, and found him, where he strode
About the hall, among his dogs, alone,
His beard a foot before him, and his hair
A yard behind. She told him of their tears,
And prayed him, 'If they pay this tax, they starve.'
Whereat he stared, replying, half-amazed,
'You would not let your little finger ache
For such as *these?*' – 'But I would die,' said she.
He laughed, and swore by Peter and by Paul:
Then filliped at the diamond in her ear;
'Oh ay, ay, ay, you talk!' – 'Alas!' she said,
'But prove me what it is I would not do.'
And from a heart as rough as Esau's hand,
He answered, 'Ride you naked through the town,
And I repeal it;' and nodding, as in scorn,
He parted, with great strides among his dogs.

So left alone, the passions of her mind,
As winds from all the compass shift and blow,
Made war upon each other for an hour,
Till pity won. She sent a herald forth,
And bade him cry, with sound of trumpet, all
The hard condition; but that she would loose
The people: therefore, as they loved her well,
From then till noon no foot should pace the street,
No eye look down, she passing; but that all
Should keep within, door shut, and window barred.

Then fled she to her inmost bower, and there
Unclasped the wedded eagles of her belt,
The grim Earl's gift; but ever at a breath
She lingered, looking like a summer moon
Half-dipt in cloud: anon she shook her head,
And showered the rippled ringlets to her knee;
Unclad herself in haste; adown the stair
Stole on; and, like a creeping sunbeam, slid
From pillar unto pillar, until she reached
The gateway; there she found her palfrey trapt
In purple blazoned with armorial gold.

Then she rode forth, clothed on with chastity:
The deep air listened round her as she rode,
And all the low wind hardly breathed for fear.
The little wide-mouthed heads upon the spout
Had cunning eyes to see: the barking cur
Made her cheek flame: her palfrey's footfall shot
Light horrors through her pulses: the blind walls
Were full of chinks and holes; and overhead
Fantastic gables, crowding, stared: but she
Not less through all bore up, till, last, she saw
The white-flowered elder-thicket from the field
Gleam through the Gothic archway in the wall.

Then she rode back, clothed on with chastity:
And one low churl, compact of thankless earth,
The fatal byword of all years to come,
Boring a little auger-hole in fear,
Peeped – but his eyes, before they had their will,
Were shrivelled into darkness in his head,
And dropt before him. So the Powers, who wait
On noble deeds, cancelled a sense misused;
And she, that knew not, passed: and all at once,
With twelve great shocks of sound, the shameless noon
Was clashed and hammered from a hundred towers,
One after one: but even then she gained
Her bower; whence reissuing, robed and crowned,
To meet her lord, she took the tax away
And built herself an everlasting name.

from *The Princess*

'Come down, O maid, from yonder mountain height:
What pleasure lives in height (the shepherd sang)
In height and cold, the splendour of the hills?
But cease to move so near the Heavens, and cease
To glide a sunbeam by the blasted Pine,
To sit a star upon the sparkling spire;
And come, for Love is of the valley, come,
For Love is of the valley, come thou down
And find him; by the happy threshold, he,
Or hand in hand with Plenty in the maize,
Or red with spirted purple of the vats,
Or foxlike in the vine; nor cares to walk
With Death and Morning on the silver horns,
Nor wilt thou snare him in the white ravine,
Nor find him dropt upon the firths of ice,
That huddling slant in furrow-cloven falls
To roll the torrent out of dusky doors:
But follow; let the torrent dance thee down
To find him in the valley; let the wild
Lean-headed Eagles yelp alone, and leave
The monstrous ledges there to slope, and spill
Their thousand wreaths of dangling water-smoke,
That like a broken purpose waste in air:
So waste not thou; but come; for all the vales
Await thee; azure pillars of the hearth
Arise to thee; the children call, and I
Thy shepherd pipe, and sweet is every sound,
Sweeter thy voice, but every sound is sweet;
Myriads of rivulets hurrying through the lawn,
The moan of doves in immemorial elms,
And murmuring of innumerable bees.'

*

'Now sleeps the crimson petal, now the white;
Nor waves the cypress in the palace walk;
Nor winks the gold fin in the porphyry font:
The fire-fly wakens: waken thou with me.

  Now droops the milkwhite peacock like a ghost,
And like a ghost she glimmers on to me.

  Now lies the Earth all Danaë to the stars,
And all thy heart lies open unto me.

  Now slides the silent meteor on, and leaves
A shining furrow, as thy thoughts in me.

  Now folds the lily all her sweetness up,
And slips into the bosom of the lake:
So fold thyself, my dearest, thou, and slip
Into my bosom and be lost in me.'

*

Ask me no more: the moon may draw the sea;
    The cloud may stoop from heaven and take the shape
    With fold to fold, of mountain or of cape;
But O too fond, when have I answered thee?
                    Ask me no more.

Ask me no more: what answer should I give?
    I love not hollow cheek or faded eye:
    Yet, O my friend, I will not have thee die!
Ask me no more, lest I should bid thee live;
                    Ask me no more.

Ask me no more: thy fate and mine are sealed:
    I strove against the stream and all in vain:
    Let the great river take me to the main:
No more, dear love, for at a touch I yield;
                    Ask me no more.

*

'Tears, idle tears, I know not what they mean,
Tears from the depth of some divine despair
Rise in the heart, and gather to the eyes,
In looking on the happy Autumn-fields,
And thinking of the days that are no more.

'Fresh as the first beam glittering on a sail,
That brings our friends up from the underworld,
Sad as the last which reddens over one
That sinks with all we love below the verge;
So sad, so fresh, the days that are no more.

'Ah, sad and strange as in dark summer dawns
The earliest pipe of half-awakened birds
To dying ears, when unto dying eyes
The casement slowly grows a glimmering square;
So sad, so strange, the days that are no more.

'Dear as remembered kisses after death,
And sweet as those by hopeless fancy feigned
On lips that are for others; deep as love,
Deep as first love, and wild with all regret;
O Death in Life, the days that are no more.'

from *In Memoriam A.H.H.*

II

Old Yew, which graspest at the stones
   That name the under-lying dead,
   Thy fibres net the dreamless head,
Thy roots are wrapt about the bones.

The seasons bring the flower again,
   And bring the firstling to the flock;
   And in the dusk of thee, the clock
Beats out the little lives of men.

O not for thee the glow, the bloom,
   Who changest not in any gale,
   Nor branding summer suns avail
To touch thy thousand years of gloom:

And gazing on thee, sullen tree,
   Sick for thy stubborn hardihood,
   I seem to fail from out my blood
And grow incorporate into thee.

V

I sometimes hold it half a sin
   To put in words the grief I feel;
   For words, like Nature, half reveal
And half conceal the Soul within.

But, for the unquiet heart and brain,
   A use in measured language lies;
   The sad mechanic exercise,
Like dull narcotics, numbing pain.

In words, like weeds, I'll wrap me o'er,
    Like coarsest clothes against the cold:
    But that large grief which these enfold
Is given in outline and no more.

VII

Dark house, by which once more I stand
    Here in the long unlovely street,
    Doors, where my heart was used to beat
So quickly, waiting for a hand,

A hand that can be clasped no more –
    Behold me, for I cannot sleep,
    And like a guilty thing I creep
At earliest morning to the door.

He is not here; but far away
    The noise of life begins again,
    And ghastly through the drizzling rain
On the bald street breaks the blank day.

XI

Calm is the morn without a sound,
    Calm as to suit a calmer grief,
    And only through the faded leaf
The chestnut pattering to the ground:

Calm and deep peace on this high wold,
    And on these dews that drench the furze,
    And all the silvery gossamers
That twinkle into green and gold:

Calm and still light on yon great plain
    That sweeps with all its autumn bowers,
    And crowded farms and lessening towers,
To mingle with the bounding main:

Calm and deep peace in this wide air,
    These leaves that redden to the fall;
    And in my heart, if calm at all,
If any calm, a calm despair:

Calm on the seas, and silver sleep,
    And waves that sway themselves in rest,
    And dead calm in that noble breast
Which heaves but with the heaving deep.

XXXI

When Lazarus left his charnel-cave,
    And home to Mary's house returned,
    Was this demanded – if he yearned
To hear her weeping by his grave?

'Where wert thou, brother, those four days?'
    There lives no record of reply,
    Which telling what it is to die
Had surely added praise to praise.

From every house the neighbours met,
    The streets were filled with joyful sound,
    A solemn gladness even crowned
The purple brows of Olivet.

Behold a man raised up by Christ!
    The rest remaineth unrevealed;
    He told it not; or something sealed
The lips of that Evangelist.

L

Be near me when my light is low,
    When the blood creeps, and the nerves prick
    And tingle; and the heart is sick,
And all the wheels of Being slow.

Be near me when the sensuous frame
    Is racked with pangs that conquer trust;
    And Time, a maniac scattering dust,
And Life, a Fury slinging flame.

Be near me when my faith is dry,
    And men the flies of latter spring,
    That lay their eggs, and sting and sing
And weave their petty cells and die.

Be near me when I fade away,
    To point the term of human strife,
    And on the low dark verge of life
The twilight of eternal day.

LIV

Oh yet we trust that somehow good
    Will be the final goal of ill,
    To pangs of nature, sins of will,
Defects of doubt, and taints of blood;

That nothing walks with aimless feet;
    That not one life shall be destroyed,
    Or cast as rubbish to the void,
When God hath made the pile complete;

That not a worm is cloven in vain;
    That not a moth with vain desire
    Is shrivelled in a fruitless fire,
Or but subserves another's gain.

Behold, we know not anything;
    I can but trust that good shall fall
    At last – far off – at last, to all,
And every winter change to spring.

So runs my dream: but what am I?
   An infant crying in the night:
   An infant crying for the light:
And with no language but a cry.

XCV

By night we lingered on the lawn,
   For underfoot the herb was dry;
   And genial warmth; and o'er the sky
The silvery haze of summer drawn;

And calm that let the tapers burn
   Unwavering: not a cricket chirred:
   The brook alone far-off was heard,
And on the board the fluttering urn:

And bats went round in fragrant skies,
   And wheeled or lit the filmy shapes
   That haunt the dusk, with ermine capes
And woolly breasts and beaded eyes;

While now we sang old songs that pealed
   From knoll to knoll, where, couched at ease,
   The white kine glimmered, and the trees
Laid their dark arms about the field.

But when those others, one by one,
   Withdrew themselves from me and night,
   And in the house light after light
Went out, and I was all alone,

A hunger seized my heart; I read
   Of that glad year which once had been,
   In those fallen leaves which kept their green,
The noble letters of the dead:

And strangely on the silence broke
The silent-speaking words, and strange
Was love's dumb cry defying change
To test his worth; and strangely spoke

The faith, the vigour, bold to dwell
On doubts that drive the coward back,
And keen through wordy snares to track
Suggestion to her inmost cell.

So word by word, and line by line,
The dead man touched me from the past,
And all at once it seemed at last
The living soul was flashed on mine,

And mine in this was wound, and whirled
About empyreal heights of thought,
And came on that which is, and caught
The deep pulsations of the world,

Æonian music measuring out
The steps of Time – the shocks of Chance –
The blows of Death. At length my trance
Was cancelled, stricken through with doubt.

Vague words! but ah, how hard to frame
In matter-moulded forms of speech,
Or even for intellect to reach
Through memory that which I became:

Till now the doubtful dusk revealed
The knolls once more where, couched at ease,
The white kine glimmered, and the trees
Laid their dark arms about the field:

And sucked from out the distant gloom
A breeze began to tremble o'er
The large leaves of the sycamore,
And fluctuate all the still perfume,

And gathering freshlier overhead,
    Rocked the full-foliaged elms, and swung
    The heavy-folded rose, and flung
The lilies to and fro, and said

'The dawn, the dawn,' and died away;
    And East and West, without a breath,
    Mixt their dim lights, like life and death,
To broaden into boundless day.

CXV

Now fades the last long streak of snow,
    Now burgeons every maze of quick
    About the flowering squares, and thick
By ashen roots the violets blow.

Now rings the woodland loud and long,
    The distance takes a lovelier hue,
    And drowned in yonder living blue
The lark becomes a sightless song.

Now dance the lights on lawn and lea,
    The flocks are whiter down the vale,
    And milkier every milky sail
On winding stream or distant sea;

Where now the seamew pipes, or dives
    In yonder greening gleam, and fly
    The happy birds, that change their sky
To build and brood; that live their lives

From land to land; and in my breast
    Spring wakens too; and my regret
    Becomes an April violet,
And buds and blossoms like the rest.

Edwin Morris
or, The Lake

O me, my pleasant rambles by the lake,
My sweet, wild, fresh three quarters of a year,
My one Oasis in the dust and drouth
Of city life! I was a sketcher then:
See here, my doing: curves of mountain, bridge,
Boat, island, ruins of a castle, built
When men knew how to build, upon a rock
With turrets lichen-gilded like a rock:
And here, new-comers in an ancient hold,
New-comers from the Mersey, millionaires,
Here lived the Hills – a Tudor-chimnied bulk
Of mellow brickwork on an isle of bowers.

O me, my pleasant rambles by the lake
With Edwin Morris and with Edward Bull
The curate; he was fatter than his cure.

But Edwin Morris, he that knew the names,
Long learnèd names of agaric, moss and fern,
Who forged a thousand theories of the rocks,
Who taught me how to skate, to row, to swim,
Who read me rhymes elaborately good,
His own – I called him Crichton, for he seemed
All-perfect, finished to the finger nail.

And once I asked him of his early life,
And his first passion; and he answered me;
And well his words became him: was he not
A full-celled honeycomb of eloquence
Stored from all flowers? Poet-like he spoke.

'My love for Nature is as old as I;
But thirty moons, one honeymoon to that,

And three rich sennights more, my love for her.
My love for Nature and my love for her,
Of different ages, like twin-sisters grew,
Twin-sisters differently beautiful.
To some full music rose and sank the sun,
And some full music seemed to move and change
With all the varied changes of the dark,
And either twilight and the day between;
For daily hope fulfilled, to rise again
Revolving toward fulfilment, made it sweet
To walk, to sit, to sleep, to wake, to breathe.'

Or this or something like to this he spoke.
Then said the fat-faced curate Edward Bull,

'I take it, God made the woman for the man,
And for the good and increase of the world.
A pretty face is well, and this is well,
To have a dame indoors, that trims us up,
And keeps us tight; but these unreal ways
Seem but the theme of writers, and indeed
Worn threadbare. Man is made of solid stuff.
I say, God made the woman for the man,
And for the good and increase of the world.'

'Parson,' said I, 'you pitch the pipe too low:
But I have sudden touches, and can run
My faith beyond my practice into his:
Though if, in dancing after Letty Hill,
I do not hear the bells upon my cap,
I scarce have other music: yet say on.
What should one give to light on such a dream?'
I asked him half-sardonically.

                                        'Give?
Give all thou art,' he answered, and a light
Of laughter dimpled in his swarthy cheek;
'I would have hid her needle in my heart,

To save her little finger from a scratch
No deeper than the skin: my ears could hear
Her lightest breath; her least remark was worth
The experience of the wise. I went and came;
Her voice fled always through the summer land;
I spoke her name alone. Thrice-happy days!
The flower of each, those moments when we met,
The crown of all, we met to part no more.'

　Were not his words delicious, I a beast
To take them as I did? but something jarred;
Whether he spoke too largely; that there seemed
A touch of something false, some self-conceit,
Or over-smoothness: howsoe'er it was,
He scarcely hit my humour, and I said:

　'Friend Edwin, do not think yourself alone
Of all men happy. Shall not Love to me,
As in the Latin song I learnt at school,
Sneeze out a full God-bless-you right and left?
But you can talk: yours is a kindly vein:
I have, I think, – Heaven knows – as much within;
Have, or should have, but for a thought or two,
That like a purple beech among the greens
Looks out of place: 'tis from no want in her:
It is my shyness, or my self-distrust,
Or something of a wayward modern mind
Dissecting passion. Time will set me right.'

　So spoke I knowing not the things that were.
Then said the fat-faced curate, Edward Bull:
'God made the woman for the use of man,
And for the good and increase of the world.'
And I and Edwin laughed; and now we paused
About the windings of the marge to hear
The soft wind blowing over meadowy holms
And alders, garden-isles; and now we left

The clerk behind us, I and he, and ran
By ripply shallows of the lisping lake,
Delighted with the freshness and the sound.

But, when the bracken rusted on their crags,
My suit had withered, nipt to death by him
That was a God, and is a lawyer's clerk,
The rentroll Cupid of our rainy isles.
'Tis true, we met; one hour I had, no more:
She sent a note, the seal an *Elle vous suit*,
The close, 'Your Letty, only yours;' and this
Thrice underscored. The friendly mist of morn
Clung to the lake. I boated over, ran
My craft aground, and heard with beating heart
The Sweet-Gale rustle round the shelving keel;
And out I stept, and up I crept: she moved,
Like Proserpine in Enna, gathering flowers:
Then low and sweet I whistled thrice; and she,
She turned, we closed, we kissed, swore faith, I breathed
In some new planet: a silent cousin stole
Upon us and departed: 'Leave,' she cried,
'O leave me!' 'Never, dearest, never: here
I brave the worst:' and while we stood like fools
Embracing, all at once a score of pugs
And poodles yelled within, and out they came
Trustees and Aunts and Uncles. 'What, with him!
Go' (shrilled the cotton-spinning chorus); 'him!'
I choked. Again they shrieked the burthen – 'Him!'
Again with hands of wild rejection 'Go! –
Girl, get you in!' She went – and in one month
They wedded her to sixty thousand pounds,
To lands in Kent and messuages in York,
And slight Sir Robert with his watery smile
And educated whisker. But for me,
They set an ancient creditor to work:
It seems I broke a close with force and arms:

There came a mystic token from the king
To greet the sheriff, needless courtesy!
I read, and fled by night, and flying turned:
Her taper glimmered in the lake below:
I turned once more, close-buttoned to the storm;
So left the place, left Edwin, nor have seen
Him since, nor heard of her, nor cared to hear.

Nor cared to hear? perhaps: yet long ago
I have pardoned little Letty; not indeed,
It may be, for her own dear sake but this,
She seems a part of those fresh days to me;
For in the dust and drouth of London life
She moves among my visions of the lake,
While the prime swallow dips his wing, or then
While the gold-lily blows, and overhead
The light cloud smoulders on the summer crag.

from Maud

Cold and clear-cut face, why come you so cruelly meek
Breaking a slumber in which all spleenful folly was drowned,
Pale with the golden beam of an eyelash dead on the cheek,
Passionless, pale, cold face, star-sweet on a gloom profound;
Womanlike, taking revenge too deep for a transient wrong
Done but in thought to your beauty, and ever as pale as before
Growing and fading and growing upon me without a sound,
Luminous, gemlike, ghostlike, deathlike, half the night long
Growing and fading and growing, till I could bear it no more,
But arose, and all by myself in my own dark garden ground,
Listening now to the tide in its broad-flung shipwrecking roar,
Now to the scream of a maddened beach dragged down by the
    wave,
Walked in a wintry wind by a ghastly glimmer, and found
The shining daffodil dead, and Orion low in his grave.

I.XVIII

I
I have led her home, my love, my only friend.
There is none like her, none.
And never yet so warmly ran my blood
And sweetly, on and on
Calming itself to the long-wished-for end,
Full to the banks, close on the promised good.

II
None like her, none.
Just now the dry-tongued laurels' pattering talk
Seemed her light foot along the garden walk,
And shook my heart to think she comes once more;

But even then I heard her close the door,
The gates of Heaven are closed, and she is gone.

III

There is none like her, none.
Nor will be when our summers have deceased.
O, art thou sighing for Lebanon
In the long breeze that streams to thy delicious East,
Sighing for Lebanon,
Dark cedar, though thy limbs have here increased,
Upon a pastoral slope as fair,
And looking to the South, and fed
With honeyed rain and delicate air,
And haunted by the starry head
Of her whose gentle will has changed my fate,
And made my life a perfumed altar-flame;
And over whom thy darkness must have spread
With such delight as theirs of old, thy great
Forefathers of the thornless garden, there
Shadowing the snow-limbed Eve from whom she came.

II.II

I

See what a lovely shell,
Small and pure as a pearl,
Lying close to my foot,
Frail, but a work divine,
Made so fairily well
With delicate spire and whorl,
How exquisitely minute,
A miracle of design!

II

What is it? a learned man
Could give it a clumsy name.

Let him name it who can,
The beauty would be the same.

III

The tiny cell is forlorn,
Void of the little living will
That made it stir on the shore.
Did he stand at the diamond door
Of his house in a rainbow frill?
Did he push, when he was uncurled,
A golden foot or a fairy horn
Through his dim water-world?

IV

Slight, to be crushed with a tap
Of my finger-nail on the sand,
Small, but a work divine,
Frail, but of force to withstand,
Year upon year, the shock
Of cataract seas that snap
The three decker's oaken spine
Athwart the ledges of rock,
Here on the Breton strand!

II.V

I

Dead, long dead,
Long dead!
And my heart is a handful of dust,
And the wheels go over my head,
And my bones are shaken with pain,
For into a shallow grave they are thrust,
Only a yard beneath the street,
And the hoofs of the horses beat, beat,
The hoofs of the horses beat,
Beat into my scalp and my brain,

With never an end to the stream of passing feet,
Driving, hurrying, marrying, burying,
Clamour and rumble, and ringing and clatter,
And here beneath it is all as bad,
For I thought the dead had peace, but it is not so;
To have no peace in the grave, is that not sad?
But up and down and to and fro,
Ever about me the dead men go;
And then to hear a dead man chatter
Is enough to drive one mad.

To the Rev. F. D. Maurice

Come, when no graver cares employ,
Godfather, come and see your boy:
   Your presence will be sun in winter,
Making the little one leap for joy.

For, being of that honest few,
Who give the Fiend himself his due,
   Should eighty-thousand college-councils
Thunder 'Anathema,' friend, at you;

Should all our churchmen foam in spite
At you, so careful of the right,
   Yet one lay-hearth would give you welcome
(Take it and come) to the Isle of Wight;

Where, far from noise and smoke of town,
I watch the twilight falling brown
   All round a careless-ordered garden
Close to the ridge of a noble down.

You'll have no scandal while you dine,
But honest talk and wholesome wine,
   And only hear the magpie gossip
Garrulous under a roof of pine:

For groves of pine on either hand,
To break the blast of winter, stand;
   And further on, the hoary Channel
Tumbles a billow on chalk and sand;

Where, if below the milky steep
Some ship of battle slowly creep,
   And on through zones of light and shadow
Glimmer away to the lonely deep,

We might discuss the Northern sin
Which made a selfish war begin;
  Dispute the claims, arrange the chances;
Emperor, Ottoman, which shall win:

Or whether war's avenging rod
Shall lash all Europe into blood;
  Till you should turn to dearer matters,
Dear to the man that is dear to God;

How best to help the slender store,
How mend the dwellings, of the poor;
  How gain in life, as life advances,
Valour and charity more and more.

Come, Maurice, come: the lawn as yet
Is hoar with rime, or spongy-wet;
  But when the wreath of March has blossomed,
Crocus, anemone, violet,

Or later, pay one visit here,
For those are few we hold as dear;
  Nor pay but one, but come for many,
Many and many a happy year.

January, 1854

from Enoch Arden

The mountain wooded to the peak, the lawns
And winding glades high up like ways to Heaven,
The slender coco's drooping crown of plumes,
The lightning flash of insect and of bird,
The lustre of the long convolvuluses
That coiled around the stately stems, and ran
Even to the limit of the land, the glows
And glories of the broad belt of the world,
All these he saw; but what he fain had seen
He could not see, the kindly human face,
Nor ever hear a kindly voice, but heard
The myriad shriek of wheeling ocean-fowl,
The league-long roller thundering on the reef,
The moving whisper of huge trees that branched
And blossomed in the zenith, or the sweep
Of some precipitous rivulet to the wave,
As down the shore he ranged, or all day long
Sat often in the seaward-gazing gorge,
A shipwrecked sailor, waiting for a sail:
No sail from day to day, but every day
The sunrise broken into scarlet shafts
Among the palms and ferns and precipices;
The blaze upon the waters to the east;
The blaze upon his island overhead;
The blaze upon the waters to the west;
Then the great stars that globed themselves in Heaven,
The hollower-bellowing ocean, and again
The scarlet shafts of sunrise – but no sail.

There often as he watched or seemed to watch,
So still, the golden lizard on him paused,
A phantom made of many phantoms moved
Before him haunting him, or he himself

Moved haunting people, things and places, known
Far in a darker isle beyond the line;
The babes, their babble, Annie, the small house,
The climbing street, the mill, the leafy lanes,
The peacock-yewtree and the lonely Hall,
The horse he drove, the boat he sold, the chill
November dawns and dewy-glooming downs,
The gentle shower, the smell of dying leaves,
And the low moan of leaden-coloured seas.

  Once likewise, in the ringing of his ears,
Though faintly, merrily – far and far away –
He heard the pealing of his parish bells;
Then, though he knew not wherefore, started up
Shuddering, and when the beauteous hateful isle
Returned upon him, had not his poor heart
Spoken with That, which being everywhere
Lets none, who speaks with Him, seem all alone,
Surely the man had died of solitude.

In the Valley of Cauteretz

All along the valley, stream that flashest white,
Deepening thy voice with the deepening of the night,
All along the valley, where thy waters flow,
I walked with one I loved two and thirty years ago.
All along the valley, while I walked today,
The two and thirty years were a mist that rolls away;
For all along the valley, down thy rocky bed,
Thy living voice to me was as the voice of the dead,
And all along the valley, by rock and cave and tree,
The voice of the dead was a living voice to me.

Northern Farmer
New Style

I

Dosn't thou 'ear my 'erse's legs, as they canters awaäy?
Proputty, proputty, proputty – that's what I 'ears 'em saäy.
Proputty, proputty, proputty – Sam, thou's an ass for thy
   paaïns:
Theer's moor sense i' one o' 'is legs nor in all thy braaïns.

II

Woä – theer's a craw to pluck wi' tha, Sam: yon's parson's
   'ouse –
Dosn't thou knaw that a man mun be eäther a man or a
   mouse?
Time to think on it then; for thou'll be twenty to weeäk.
Proputty, proputty – woä then woä – let ma 'ear mysén speäk.

III

Me an' thy muther, Sammy, 'as beän a-talkin' o' thee;
Thou's beän talkin' to muther, an' she beän a tellin' it me.
Thou'll not marry for munny – thou's sweet upo' parson's
   lass –
Noä – thou'll marry for luvv – an' we boäth on us thinks tha an
   ass.

IV

Seeä'd her todaäy goä by – Saäint's-daäy – they was ringing the
   bells.
She's a beauty thou thinks – an' soä is scoors o' gells,
Them as 'as munny an' all – wot's a beauty? – the flower as
   blaws.
But proputty, proputty sticks, an' proputty, proputty graws.

V

Do'ant be stunt: taäke time: I knaws what maäkes tha sa mad.
Warn't I craäzed fur the lasses mysén when I wur a lad?

55

But I knawed a Quaäker feller as often 'as towd ma this:
'Doänt thou marry for munny, but goä wheer munny is!'

VI

An' I went wheer munny war: an' thy muther coom to 'and,
Wi' lots o' munny laaïd by, an' a nicetish bit o' land.
Maäybe she warn't a beauty: – I niver giv it a thowt –
But warn't she as good to cuddle an' kiss as a lass as 'ant nowt?

VII

Parson's lass 'ant nowt, an' she weänt 'a nowt when 'e's deäd,
Mun be a guvness, lad, or summut, and addle her breäd:
Why? fur 'e's nobbut a curate, an' weänt niver git hissen clear,
An' 'e maäde the bed as 'e ligs on afoor 'e coomed to the shere.

VIII

An' thin 'e coomed to the parish wi' lots o' Varsity debt,
Stook to his taaïl they did, an' 'e 'ant got shut on 'em yet.
An' 'e ligs on 'is back i' the grip, wi' noän to lend 'im a shuvv,
Woorse nor a far-weltered yowe: fur, Sammy, 'e married fur
    luvv.

IX

Luvv? what's luvv? thou can luvv thy lass an' 'er munny too,
Maakin' 'em goä togither as they've good right to do.
Could'n I luvv thy muther by cause o' 'er munny laaïd by?
Naäy – fur I luvved 'er a vast sight moor fur it: reäson why.

X

Ay an' thy muther says thou wants to marry the lass,
Cooms of a gentleman burn: an' we boäth on us think tha an
    ass.
Woä then, proputty, wiltha? – an ass as near as mays nowt –
Woä then, wiltha? dangtha! – the bees is as fell as owt.

XI

Breäk me a bit o' the esh for his 'eäd lad, out o' the fence!
Gentleman burn! what's gentleman burn? is it shillins an'
  pence?
Proputty, proputty's ivrything 'ere, an', Sammy, I'm blest
If it isn't the saäme oop yonder, fur them as 'as it's the best.

XII

Tis'n them as 'as munny as breaks into 'ouses an' steäls,
Them as 'as coäts to their backs an' taäkes their regular meäls.
Noä, but it's them as niver knaws wheer a meal's to be 'ad.
Taäke my word for it, Sammy, the poor in a loomp is bad.

XIII

Them or thir feythers, tha sees, mun 'a beän a laäzy lot,
Fur work mun 'a gone to the gittin' whiniver munny was got.
Feyther 'ad ammost nowt; leästways 'is munny was 'id.
But 'e tued an' moiled 'issén deäd, an 'e died a good un, 'e did.

XIV

Look thou theer wheer Wrigglesby beck cooms out by the 'ill!
Feyther run oop to the farm, an' I runs oop to the mill;
An' I'll run oop to the brig, an' that thou'll live to see;
And if thou marries a good un I'll leäve the land to thee.

XV

Thim's my noätions, Sammy, wheerby I means to stick;
But if thou marries a bad un, I'll leäve the land to Dick.–
Coom oop, proputty, proputty – that's what I 'ears 'im saäy –
Proputty, proputty, proputty – canter an' canter awaäy.

from The Voyage of Maeldune

And we came to the Silent Isle that we never had touched at
  before,
Where a silent ocean always broke on a silent shore,
And the brooks glittered on in the light without sound, and the
  long waterfalls
Poured in a thunderless plunge to the base of the mountain
  walls,
And the poplar and cypress unshaken by storm flourished up
  beyond sight,
And the pine shot aloft from the crag to an unbelievable
  height,
And high in the heaven above it there flickered a songless lark,
And the cock couldn't crow, and the bull couldn't low, and the
  dog couldn't bark.
And round it we went, and through it, but never a murmur, a
  breath –
It was all of it fair as life, it was all of it quiet as death,
And we hated the beautiful Isle, for whenever we strove to
  speak
Our voices were thinner and fainter than any flittermouse-
  shriek;
And the men that were mighty of tongue and could raise such
  a battle-cry
That a hundred who heard it would rush on a thousand lances
  and die –
O they to be dumbed by the charm! – so flustered with anger
  were they
They almost fell on each other; but after we sailed away.

And we came to the Isle of Shouting, we landed, a score of wild
  birds

Cried from the topmost summit with human voices and
  words;

Once in an hour they cried, and whenever their voices pealed

The steer fell down at the plow and the harvest died from the
  field,

And the men dropt dead in the valleys and half of the cattle
  went lame,

And the roof sank in on the hearth, and the dwelling broke
  into flame;

And the shouting of these wild birds ran into the hearts of my
  crew,

Till they shouted along with the shouting and seized one
  another and slew;

But I drew them the one from the other; I saw that we could
  not stay,

And we left the dead to the birds and we sailed with our
  wounded away.

Rizpah

I

Wailing, wailing, wailing, the wind over land and sea –
And Willy's voice in the wind, 'O mother, come out to me.'
Why should he call me tonight, when he knows that I cannot
    go?
For the downs are as bright as day, and the full moon stares at
    the snow.

II

We should be seen, my dear; they would spy us out of the
    town.
The loud black nights for us, and the storm rushing over the
    down,
When I cannot see my own hand, but am led by the creak of
    the chain,
And grovel and grope for my son till I find myself drenched
    with the rain.

III

Anything fallen again? nay – what was there left to fall?
I have taken them home, I have numbered the bones, I have
    hidden them all.
What am I saying? and what are *you*? do you come as a spy?
Falls? what falls? who knows? As the tree falls so must it lie.

IV

Who let her in? how long has she been? you – what have you
    heard?
Why did you sit so quiet? you never have spoken a word.
O – to pray with me – yes – a lady – none of their spies –
But the night has crept into my heart, and begun to darken my
    eyes.

V

Ah – you, that have lived so soft, what should *you* know of the night,
The blast and the burning shame and the bitter frost and the fright?
I have done it, while you were asleep – you were only made for the day.
I have gathered my baby together – and now you may go your way.

VI

Nay – for it's kind of you, Madam, to sit by an old dying wife.
But say nothing hard of my boy, I have only an hour of life.
I kissed my boy in the prison, before he went out to die.
'They dared me to do it,' he said, and he never has told me a lie.
I whipt him for robbing an orchard once when he was but a child –
'The farmer dared me to do it,' he said; he was always so wild –
And idle – and couldn't be idle – my Willy – he never could rest.
The King should have made him a soldier, he would have been one of his best.

VII

But he lived with a lot of wild mates, and they never would let him be good;
They swore that he dare not rob the mail, and he swore that he would;
And he took no life, but he took one purse, and when all was done
He flung it among his fellows – I'll none of it, said my son.

VIII

I came into court to the Judge and the lawyers. I told them my
tale,
God's own truth – but they killed him, they killed him for
robbing the mail.
They hanged him in chains for a show – we had always borne a
good name –
To be hanged for a thief – and then put away – isn't that
enough shame?
Dust to dust – low down – let us hide! but they set him so high
That all the ships of the world could stare at him, passing by.
God 'ill pardon the hell-black raven and horrible fowls of the
air,
But not the black heart of the lawyer who killed him and
hanged him there.

IX

And the jailer forced me away. I had bid him my last goodbye;
They had fastened the door of his cell. 'O mother!' I heard him
cry.
I couldn't get back though I tried, he had something further to
say,
And now I never shall know it. The jailer forced me away.

X

Then since I couldn't but hear that cry of my boy that was
dead,
They seized me and shut me up: they fastened me down on my
bed.
'Mother, O mother!' – he called in the dark to me year after
year –
They beat me for that, they beat me – you know that I couldn't
but hear;
And then at the last they found I had grown so stupid and still
They let me abroad again – but the creatures had worked their
will.

XI

Flesh of my flesh was gone, but bone of my bone was left –
I stole them all from the lawyers – and you, will you call it a
    theft? –
My baby, the bones that had sucked me, the bones that had
    laughed and had cried –
Theirs? O no! they are mine – not theirs – they had moved in
    my side.

XII

Do you think I was scared by the bones? I kissed 'em, I buried
    'em all –
I can't dig deep, I am old – in the night by the churchyard wall.
My Willy 'ill rise up whole when the trumpet of judgment 'ill
    sound,
But I charge you never to say that I laid him in holy ground.

XIII

They would scratch him up – they would hang him again on
    the cursèd tree.
Sin? O yes – we are sinners, I know – let all that be,
And read me a Bible verse of the Lord's good will toward men –
'Full of compassion and mercy, the Lord' – let me hear it again;
'Full of compassion and mercy – long-suffering.' Yes, O yes!
For the lawyer is born but to murder – the Saviour lives but to
    bless.
He'll never put on the black cap except for the worst of the
    worst,
And the first may be last – I have heard it in church –and the
    last may be first.
Suffering – O long-suffering – yes, as the Lord must know,
Year after year in the mist and the wind and the shower and
    the snow.

Heard, have you? what? they have told you he never repented
his sin.

How do they know it? are *they* his mother? are *you* of his kin?

Heard! have you ever heard, when the storm on the downs
began,

The wind that 'ill wail like a child and the sea that 'ill moan like
a man?

XV

Election, Election and Reprobation – it's all very well.

But I go tonight to my boy, and I shall not find him in Hell.

For I cared so much for my boy that the Lord has looked into
my care,

And He means me I'm sure to be happy with Willy, I know not
where.

XVI

And if *he* be lost – but to save *my* soul that is all your desire:

Do you think that I care for *my* soul if my boy be gone to the
fire?

I have been with God in the dark – go, go, you may leave me
alone –

You never have borne a child – you are just as hard as a stone.

XVII

Madam, I beg your pardon! I think that you mean to be kind,

But I cannot hear what you say for my Willy's voice in the
wind –

The snow and the sky so bright – he used but to call in the
dark,

And he calls to me now from the church and not from the
gibbet – for hark!

Nay – you can hear it yourself – it is coming – shaking the
walls –

Willy – the moon's in a cloud – Good-night. I am going. He
calls.

To E. FitzGerald

Old Fitz, who from your suburb grange,
  Where once I tarried for a while,
Glance at the wheeling Orb of change,
  And greet it with a kindly smile;
Whom yet I see as there you sit
  Beneath your sheltering garden-tree,
And while your doves about you flit,
  And plant on shoulder, hand and knee,
Or on your head their rosy feet,
  As if they knew your diet spares
Whatever moved in that full sheet
  Let down to Peter at his prayers;
Who live on milk and meal and grass;
  And once for ten long weeks I tried
Your table of Pythagoras,
  And seemed at first 'a thing enskied'
(As Shakespeare has it) airy-light
  To float above the ways of men,
Then fell from that half-spiritual height
  Chilled, till I tasted flesh again
One night when earth was winter-black,
  And all the heavens flashed in frost;
And on me, half-asleep, came back
  That wholesome heat the blood had lost,
And set me climbing icy capes
  And glaciers, over which there rolled
To meet me long-armed vines with grapes
  Of Eshcol hugeness; for the cold
Without, and warmth within me, wrought
  To mould the dream; but none can say
That Lenten fare makes Lenten thought,
  Who reads your golden Eastern lay,
Than which I know no version done

In English more divinely well;
A planet equal to the sun
   Which cast it, that large infidel
Your Omar; and your Omar drew
   Full-handed plaudits from our best
In modern letters, and from two,
   Old friends outvaluing all the rest,
Two voices heard on earth no more;
   But we old friends are still alive,
And I am nearing seventy-four,
   While you have touched at seventy-five,
And so I send a birthday line
   Of greeting; and my son, who dipt
In some forgotten book of mine
   With sallow scraps of manuscript,
And dating many a year ago,
   Has hit on this, which you will take
My Fitz, and welcome, as I know
   Less for its own than for the sake
Of one recalling gracious times,
   When, in our younger London days,
You found some merit in my rhymes,
   And I more pleasure in your praise.

*

'One height and one far-shining fire'
   And while I fancied that my friend
For this brief idyll would require
   A less diffuse and opulent end,
And would defend his judgment well,
   If I should deem it over nice –
The tolling of his funeral bell
   Broke on my Pagan Paradise,
And mixt the dreams of classic times,
   And all the phantoms of the dream,
With present grief, and made the rhymes,

That missed his living welcome, seem
Like would-be guests an hour too late,
   Who down the highway moving on
With easy laughter find the gate
   Is bolted, and the master gone.
Gone into darkness, that full light
   Of friendship! past, in sleep, away
By night, into the deeper night!
   The deeper night? A clearer day
Than our poor twilight dawn on earth –
   If night, what barren toil to be!
What life, so maimed by night, were worth
   Our living out? Not mine to me
Remembering all the golden hours
   Now silent, and so many dead,
And him the last; and laying flowers,
   This wreath, above his honoured head,
And praying that, when I from hence
   Shall fade with him into the unknown,
My close of earth's experience
   May prove as peaceful as his own.

from Merlin and Vivien

Scarce had she ceased, when out of heaven a bolt
(For now the storm was close above them) struck,
Furrowing a giant oak, and javelining
With darted spikes and splinters of the wood
The dark earth round. He raised his eyes and saw
The tree that shone white-listed through the gloom.
But Vivien, fearing heaven had heard her oath,
And dazzled by the livid-flickering fork,
And deafened with the stammering cracks and claps
That followed, flying back and crying out,
'O Merlin, though you do not love me, save,
Yet save me!' clung to him and hugged him close;
And called him dear protector in her fright,
Nor yet forgot her practice in her fright,
But wrought upon his mood and hugged him close.
The pale blood of the wizard at her touch
Took gayer colours, like an opal warmed.
She blamed herself for telling hearsay tales:
She shook from fear, and for her fault she wept
Of petulancy; she called him lord and liege,
Her seer, her bard, her silver star of eve,
Her God, her Merlin, the one passionate love
Of her whole life; and ever overhead
Bellowed the tempest, and the rotten branch
Snapt in the rushing of the river-rain
Above them; and in change of glare and gloom
Her eyes and neck glittering went and came;
Till now the storm, its burst of passion spent,
Moaning and calling out of other lands,
Had left the ravaged woodland yet once more

To peace; and what should not have been had been,
For Merlin, overtalked and overworn,
Had yielded, told her all the charm, and slept.

from The Last Tournament

But when the morning of a tournament,
By these in earnest those in mockery called
The Tournament of the Dead Innocence,
Brake with a wet wind blowing, Lancelot,
Round whose sick head all night, like birds of prey,
The words of Arthur flying shrieked, arose,
And down a streetway hung with folds of pure
White samite, and by fountains running wine,
Where children sat in white with cups of gold,
Moved to the lists, and there, with slow sad steps
Ascending, filled his double-dragoned chair.

He glanced and saw the stately galleries,
Dame, damsel, each through worship of their Queen
White-robed in honour of the stainless child,
And some with scattered jewels, like a bank
Of maiden snow mingled with sparks of fire.
He looked but once, and vailed his eyes again.

The sudden trumpet sounded as in a dream
To ears but half-awaked, then one low roll
Of Autumn thunder, and the jousts began:
And ever the wind blew, and yellowing leaf
And gloom and gleam, and shower and shorn plume
Went down it. Sighing weariedly, as one
Who sits and gazes on a faded fire,
When all the goodlier guests are past away,
Sat their great umpire, looking o'er the lists.
He saw the laws that ruled the tournament
Broken, but spake not; once, a knight cast down
Before his throne of arbitration cursed
The dead babe and the follies of the King;

And once the laces of a helmet cracked,
And showed him, like a vermin in its hole,
Modred, a narrow face ...

from Guinevere

But when Sir Lancelot told
This matter to the Queen, at first she laughed
Lightly, to think of Modred's dusty fall,
Then shuddered, as the village wife who cries
'I shudder, some one steps across my grave;'
Then laughed again, but faintlier, for indeed
She half-foresaw that he, the subtle beast,
Would track her guilt until he found, and hers
Would be for evermore a name of scorn.
Henceforward rarely could she front in hall,
Or elsewhere, Modred's narrow foxy face,
Heart-hiding smile, and gray persistent eye:
Henceforward too, the Powers that tend the soul,
To help it from the death that cannot die,
And save it even in extremes, began
To vex and plague her. Many a time for hours,
Beside the placid breathings of the King,
In the dead night, grim faces came and went
Before her, or a vague spiritual fear –
Like to some doubtful noise of creaking doors,
Heard by the watcher in a haunted house,
That keeps the rust of murder on the walls –
Held her awake: or if she slept, she dreamed
An awful dream; for then she seemed to stand
On some vast plain before a setting sun,
And from the sun there swiftly made at her
A ghastly something, and its shadow flew
Before it, till it touched her, and she turned –
When lo! her own, that broadening from her feet,
And blackening, swallowed all the land, and in it
Far cities burnt, and with a cry she woke.

from The Passing of Arthur

Then rose the King and moved his host by night,
And ever pushed Sir Modred, league by league,
Back to the sunset bound of Lyonnesse —
A land of old upheaven from the abyss
By fire, to sink into the abyss again;
Where fragments of forgotten peoples dwelt,
And the long mountains ended in a coast
Of ever-shifting sand, and far away
The phantom circle of a moaning sea.
There the pursuer could pursue no more,
And he that fled no further fly the King;
And there, that day when the great light of heaven
Burned at his lowest in the rolling year,
On the waste sand by the waste sea they closed.
Nor ever yet had Arthur fought a fight
Like this last, dim, weird battle of the west.
A deathwhite mist slept over sand and sea:
Whereof the chill, to him who breathed it, drew
Down with his blood, till all his heart was cold
With formless fear; and even on Arthur fell
Confusion, since he saw not whom he fought.
For friend and foe were shadows in the mist,
And friend slew friend not knowing whom he slew;
And some had visions out of golden youth,
And some beheld the faces of old ghosts
Look in upon the battle; and in the mist
Was many a noble deed, many a base,
And chance and craft and strength in single fights,
And ever and anon with host to host
Shocks, and the splintering spear, the hard mail hewn,
Shield-breakings, and the clash of brands, the crash
Of battleaxes on shattered helms, and shrieks
After the Christ, of those who falling down

Looked up for heaven, and only saw the mist;
And shouts of heathen and the traitor knights,
Oaths, insult, filth, and monstrous blasphemies,
Sweat, writhings, anguish, labouring of the lungs
In that close mist, and cryings for the light,
Moans of the dying, and voices of the dead.

Last, as by some one deathbed after wail
Of suffering, silence follows, or through death
Or deathlike swoon, thus over all that shore,
Save for some whisper of the seething seas,
A dead hush fell; but when the dolorous day
Grew drearier toward twilight falling, came
A bitter wind, clear from the North, and blew
The mist aside, and with that wind the tide
Rose, and the pale King glanced across the field
Of battle: but no man was moving there;
Nor any cry of Christian heard thereon,
Nor yet of heathen; only the wan wave
Brake in among dead faces, to and fro
Swaying the helpless hands, and up and down
Tumbling the hollow helmets of the fallen,
And shivered brands that once had fought with Rome,
And rolling far along the gloomy shores
The voice of days of old and days to be.

To the Marquis of Dufferin and Ava

I

At times our Britain cannot rest,
    At times her steps are swift and rash;
    She moving, at her girdle clash
The golden keys of East and West.

II

Not swift or rash, when late she lent
    The sceptres of her West, her East,
    To one, that ruling has increased
Her greatness and her self-content.

III

Your rule has made the people love
    Their ruler. Your viceregal days
    Have added fulness to the phrase
Of 'Gauntlet in the velvet glove.'

IV

But since your name will grow with Time,
    Not all, as honouring your fair fame
    Of Statesman, have I made the name
A golden portal to my rhyme:

V

But more, that you and yours may know
    From me and mine, how dear a debt
    We owed you, and are owing yet
To you and yours, and still would owe.

VI

For he – your India was his Fate,
    And drew him over sea to you –
    He fain had ranged her through and through,
To serve her myriads and the State, –

A soul that, watched from earliest youth,
   And on through many a brightening year,
   Had never swerved for craft or fear,
By one side-path, from simple truth;

Who might have chased and claspt Renown
   And caught her chaplet here – and there
   In haunts of jungle-poisoned air
The flame of life went wavering down;

But ere he left your fatal shore,
   And lay on that funereal boat,
   Dying, 'Unspeakable' he wrote
'Their kindness,' and he wrote no more;

And sacred is the latest word;
   And now the Was, the Might-have-been,
   And those lone rites I have not seen,
And one drear sound I have not heard,

Are dreams that scarce will let me be,
   Not there to bid my boy farewell,
   When That within the coffin fell,
Fell – and flashed into the Red Sea,

Beneath a hard Arabian moon
   And alien stars. To question, why
   The sons before the fathers die,
Not mine! and I may meet him soon;

XIII

But while my life's late eve endures,
   Nor settles into hueless gray,
   My memories of his briefer day
Will mix with love for you and yours.

Crossing the Bar

Sunset and evening star,
   And one clear call for me!
And may there be no moaning of the bar,
   When I put out to sea,

But such a tide as moving seems asleep,
   Too full for sound and foam,
When that which drew from out the boundless deep
   Turns again home.

Twilight and evening bell,
   And after that the dark!
And may there be no sadness of farewell,
   When I embark;

For though from out our bourne of Time and Place
   The flood may bear me far,
I hope to see my Pilot face to face
   When I have crost the bar.